SUDDENLY, ALL HELL BROKE LOOSE!!!

pictureshowpress.net

Grateful acknowledgements to the publications where these poems first appeared: *Dirt Bag Review, Heartbreak Anthology, Misfit Magazine, Nerve Cowboy, Redshift 2, Unsheathed: 24 Contemporary Poets Take Up the Knife, V: An Anthology of Poetry*, and *Vamp Cat*.

Cover art: Alexander Grahovsky

FIRST EDITION

ISBN-13: 978-1-7341702-0-7
ISBN-10: 1-7341702-0-4

SUDDENLY, ALL HELL BROKE LOOSE!!!

Poems

BRIAN HARMAN

Picture Show Press

For the poets, non-poets, highbrowers, lowbrowers, humorists, sad saps, music geeks, book lovers, pop culture fans, buffs, muffs, office workers, couch potatoes, adventurous at heart, this is for you. To my Mom, please read only pages...1, 3, 15-18, 29, 39-40, 44-45.

POEMS

Satan's Bacon

You would think	bacon
would have been the apple on the tree,	
the forbidden meat,	
the crispy temptation,	
for nothing is as pure sin,	
sex is makin'	bacon,
money is bringing home the	bacon,
when you save someone's	bacon,
pull it out of a fire and ask	
what was it doing there in the first place?	
I can tell you what's shakin',	bacon,
	bacon
makes everything taste better,	
the scent alone has you salivating	
like a cartoon wolf,	
the way it sizzles in its own	
strip tease of grease,	
one hot orgy you want to be a part of,	
but get too close and you will feel	
its stinging spatter. So, you wait,	
as the fat burns and shrinks,	
you wonder if you're making	
the right decision for your body,	
for your body is the temple,	
remember? And you believe	
the lettuce and tomato	
will be your salvation,	
that draining the pan and patting the	bacon
with a paper towel is going to	
deliver you from evil,	
and calories, and becoming what you eat,	
and maybe what you already are—	
if you are not cured from	bacon,
will you sprout your wings for the coming	
apocalypse?	

Groundhog Philosophy

Even the groundhog is in its hole
channeling a sentient what the fuck,
another February 2nd,
another fat yawn,
another town summoning,
another poking a head out,
another 39% accurate weather prediction,
sunny, cloudy, shadow, no shadow,
same Pennsylvania,
same Punxsutawney,
same Gobbler's Knob,
even the groundhog is hitting
the snooze button, is begging
somebody to bring the mallet
or stick a dick in the hole,
stir it up already,
blow up another golf course,
meet up for tequila sunrises at the 19th,
even the groundhog walks into a bar
for a change, doesn't give a fuck about
how much chuck could a woodchuck chuck,
a marmot deciding the fate of the seasons,
no more leaving it to the land beaver,
no more predeterminism,
no more definition of crazy,
put an end to the mulligan shenanigans,
the wild grass is calling,
the berries are in the bushes,
the birds and bees are hornier than ever,
say goodbye to hibernation,
say goodbye to fetches,
say goodbye to Bill Murray again and again.

Ratt Revelations

Ratt music is built upon rat tendencies,
lewd human behavior, lay it down,
back for more, body talk,
out of the cellar, round and round
clichés, it's not exactly poetry,
in poetry, expressing in clichés
is like finding rat droppings in a fancy
restaurant, but it happens, it happens
far too often out on the street,
where we meet in lounges, in coffee
shops, in print, a cliché just
doesn't work by itself, because,
and because is a dirty word too,
it doesn't go beneath the surface,
it doesn't go back into the cellar
where you find the dark origins
of humanity, if I was to amplify
what comes around goes around,
would you tell me why, would
your fingers break into the air
like a guitar hero, would you bang
your head, even if it's against the wall,
would you be open to Ratt's poetic
rebellion becoming an exception
to the rule, how hair metal nostalgia
begets a hair metal poem, how
in an underground club you dance
looking for love but come to find
out you were somehow related,
not in the way Milton Berle
was the actual uncle of the band's
manager, but if you discovered
fossils were unearthed in China,
that what is now called a Super Rat
rocked it with the dinosaurs

over a hundred million years ago,
is considered to be the earliest known
ancestor of mammals, think about
our front teeth, think about how
our hair becomes ratted, think
about our beady eyes, our sneak,
our survival instinct, our nocturnal
sensibilities, think about our mass
reproduction, our lab breakthroughs,
our brain design is a maze,
how we're so caught up
in the rat race, how we rationalize,
rat-a-tat-tat you dirty rat,
how we just don't give a rat's ass,
think about the Year of the Rat being
the first of all Chinese Zodiac animals,
how we feel like a rat in a cage,
social cannibalism, Ratatouille,
the Mickey Mouse production
of An American Tail's theme song,
somewhere out there a rat is bruxing,
think about our cheese addiction,
how you can't wait to nibble on
a slice of cheddar, on an eighties piece
of cheesy music, on your lover's
slip of the lip when the sun goes down.

Work Sucks

The alarm goes off at 5 fucking a.m., wakes me from a dream of falling from a cliff into rapid arm movement for the snooze button, my ten-minute chance to plummet again in high hopes of hitting the ground before hearing once more, the thing I hate most in this world, TIME, plugged in to the wall socket, telling me to get my ass out of bed, so I can stub my toe on the dresser, so I can drop the soap in the shower, so I can nick my neck in the mirror, so I can stare sadly into my closet of nothing to wear, so I can get toothpaste on my shirt, so I can dig my keys out of the dirty laundry, so I can spill scalding hot coffee on my hand along the dewy duck quack walk to the car, so I can drive to red light after red light just to get to the red brake lights of the gridlocked freeway, so I can grip the steering wheel road rage tight on the verge to another aneurism, call somebody an idiot, a stupid bitch, a fuck face, a piece of shit cocksucker, so I can change lanes and end up in the only lane that isn't moving, so that after an hour of stop-and-go I can pull in to a space in the BFE zone of the office parking lot barely big enough for a dumb ass Smart car, so I can scamper up the stairs past the million dollar statue of a naked goddess twirling ribbons with bird turd on her shoulders, just to get held up by Bob the security guy who needs to see my keyfob for the hundredth time, so I can make it to my desk again late with looks that can kill from maybe Death herself, boss Lorna, so I can sit and swivel in my windowless cubicle and attempt to check eight thousand voice messages as phones are ringing around me like a charity marathon, so I can say screw this and "pretend" like I'm working by having a conversation with the dial tone while running my fingers over the keyboard like Billy Joel is in a piano duel with Elton John, so I can pull out a pack of candy cigarettes and take smoke breaks every ten minutes with the rest of the chain smokers, so that by lunch time I can go sleep in my hot car and come back with bed head, so I can pretend I have food poisoning and make a mad dash for the bathroom like I have a sudden case of the loosey gooseys. Now, that's what I call multitasking! That's the way to cope with files stacking up to the rain-stained ceiling, with unpaid overtime, with threats of being put on "problem solution," with fax machine errors, copier jams, paper cuts, ink blots, computer glitches, memos, emails, gossip queens, stalkers, I.T. nerds, dandruff, B.O., smelly breath, rock hard bagels, cafeteria coffee that tastes like caffeinated toilet water. And not to forget to mention, the secretary is a fat, sweaty, convicted child molester, the department manager Ken is a giant ass pimple, my immediate supervisor is a backstabbing bitch, and my drive home from work is a creeping, crawling, concrete suicide that sends me straight to the couch, scratching my nut sack in front of the TV, comatose, which leads me into tomorrow morning, when my alarm is accidentally deactivated, when I wake when I want and call out sick for the rest of my goddamn life.

Road Words

Everyday, more and more on the road,
not jazz riff, cool breeze, Bebop,
scat cat Kerouac types, more like
dickwad, dipshit, asshole, motherfucker,
cunt, bitch, twat, skank, prick,
tailgating tallywacker, turkey butts,
as my mom would call them,
weavers and cutters, like they think
they're evil Disney Dalmatian fur coat
wearers, on certain days, dependent
upon my fuse, I'll slow way down,
tap the brakes, tap-tap-tap and look back
with psychotic rearview eyes, a game
of karmic dickery, those dunce drivers
tend to not like that, but karma
is a you know what, I'll see a bird
without feathers fly from a window,
and out from mine, my finger is already
perched, gesturing a parroted fuck you,
fuck you too Polly, I'm just trying
to get from point A to point B
without a propositional fallacy
screwing it all up, sometimes, I wish
I had spikes on my wheels to grind
away at their Mercedes, or release
tacks from the undercarriage like
an arcade spy game, pop their tires
and watch them swerve into a ditch
and die, how those sons of bitches
deserve it, but at the end of the day,
what I should really do is suction cup
a Baby On Board sign or slap on
a Keep Calm and Honk If You're
Horny bumper sticker, drive below
the speed limit with the top down,
smile and wave, hey, I'm horny
too, pull over and blow me.

Burning Lust

In the car next
to mine, stopped
at a traffic light,
a woman takes
a long drag.
I've got my hands
at ten and two,
imagining
reincarnation
as a cigarette—
me between her
fingers, her moist
lips, her filthy
lungs sucking
my smoke
down her throat.
It excites me
to think
a woman can buzz,
feel calm and sexy
from my chemical
affection.
As I burn
in her mouth,
I need her to finish
before the light
changes,
the blow
of my filtered
smoke circling
the inside of her
vehicle,
my scent
permeating
her body.

#FoodPorn

this bacon date sizzle,
this chocolate eclair,
this fondue fountain,
this pepperoni big slice,
this open bag of Doritos,
this Voodoo Donut box,
this Animal Style In-N-Out burger,
this tapas, paella, sangria,
this gastropub truffle fries,
this green pea toast & edible gladiolus,
this organic Rumi Latte,
this pink, Hemingway Daiquiri,
this Margrite self portrait,
this Arcimboldo Vertumnus painting,
this Nyotaimori, body sushi,
this SPAM carved ampersand,
this Moons Over My Hammy,
this All-You-Can-Eat Treasure Island Buffet,
this Hooters bone-in wings basket,
this 24-hour Wienerschnitzel,
this carrot top, not the magician,
this growing cucumbers Martha Stewart trick,
this eggplant emoji sext,
this Pringles duck lips selfie,
this summer sausage in January,
this corn cob typewriter, circle technique,
this tri-tip, even if it's just the tip, sandwich,
this orchard festival wet bob for Jazz apples,
this Herb Alpert Whipped Cream
& Other Delights stained album cover,
this curved banana split, tongue-tied
cherry stem on a Neapolitan bedspread,
this half-bitten Twinkie,
this milkshake brings all the boys to the yard,
and they're like,

this bus stop lollipop,
this fluffer crêpe,
this street taco on Hollywood and Vine,
this Elmore Leonard-inspired moist cupcake poem,
this nut butter on lady fingers,
this balsamic vinaigrette tossed salad,
this lovely little cumquat tree,
this Early Girl tomato squirt,
this spotted dick can,
this head cheese on Pumpernickel,
this Cream of Sum Yung Gai,
this Oolong tea bag,
this meatball sub all covered with marinara,
this Bachelorette Party penis popper,
this mathematical formula for consuming pie,
this pound cake, the day after,
this vodka-infused watermelon baby shower,
this FOOD HAS REPLACED SEX, NOW
I CAN'T EVEN GET INTO MY OWN PANTS meme,
this baked chocolate bells instead
of Hershey's Kisses Christmas nipple cookies,
this bent over peach in the open light
of a fully-loaded beer fridge,
this naked man cooking for you in nothing, but
an I'M HERE TO SERVE YOU TONIGHT apron,
this glossy fire BBQ sauce
that could be a clever name for a lipstick color
of a rimmed mouth,
this strawberry feed to a blindfold on knees,
this image of Eve still reaching for forbidden fruit
with a serpent snaking paradisal, curvaceous hips,
this Coney Island, Nathan's Hot Dog Eating Contest,
Koboyashi-Chestnut jowl movement record
photo finish.

Book Lovers

are misnomered, are really,
how shall I put this,
book perverts,
feen for racy romance covers,
fetish for Penguin, arouse feels
at festivals, wink at poetry readings,
tingle from the inkling of the next
novel idea, fondle anything,
anytime, anywhere there is
book association, it doesn't matter,
24/7 dogeared book lust,
rise with The Golden Apples of
the Sun, also rises to Hemingway,
to a.m. coffee in mugs with pert
sayings like, I Like Big Books
and I Can Not Lie, or I'm a
Read or Die Bitch, sport morning
wood for Norwegian Wood,
play detective to the fridge
after a big sleep, hard boiled eggs,
pulp mimosas, Wheaties
in nothing but underwear, the oh
so clever allusion of a breakfast
of champions before a naked lunch,
all sprawled out on a down feather
duvet, petting spines and pussycats,
pages spread eagle, nose deep
in the shaved papyrus of a perfumed
forest, mouth wide open with
next chapter anticipation, a clockwork
drool caught in a time machine,
preface to the afterthought,
online or bookstore, a present day
Catch-22, out of the house
ushering Edgar Allan Poe socks,

1984 canvas bag, to the local brick
and mortar to flirt with baristas,
stay perky fantasizing at café tables,
vanilla iced-lattes, maple walnut
muffins, side stacks of curiosities:
Why Do Men Have Nipples?,
The Sex Lives of Cannibals,
Tequila Mockingbird, Oral Sadism
and the Vegetarian Personality, How
to Make Damn Ass Good Artisan
Sourdough Bread, The Complete
Works of Henry Wadsworth
Longfellow, book perverts with
lusty reads in musty corners,
sporadic titter in Erotica, eyes
peeking in Mystery over Fiction
into Travel, shameless, public
displays of kindle-lipped air-reading
brushed against Psychology
bookshelves, psychoanalyze Freud
into Moby-Dick innuendos, head
back to the car to get off at the local
library, to peruse more free books
and free looks at sexy librarians,
scan periodically in Periodicals,
preference in Reference, an off
chance to find a Romeo or Juliet
who could conjecture upon S&M
theories of the Shakespearean collar,
hand cramps back at search counters,
hummingbird finger of mouse clicks
and pencil thrusts of jotting down
call numbers like 3.14Kant,
.069Cummings on scraps to become
markers that slide into stamped
and dated check-outs, a book orgy
to pile on the cherry-stained table,
to grab and lounge on the velvet,

eggplant sofa, Cheshire cat
rubbing at the reading lamp,
purring for attention, to be fancy fed,
to be stroked, to curl up, and listen;
book perverts also make avid
alcohol perverts.

Sexy Dwarf (Fairytale of the 8th)

Sexy slips into Snow White's bed at night,
when she's sleeping like Sleeping Beauty,
when she's wearing her tight lace bodice
her stepmother gave her, when she's in mid-
dream, not a dream-wish her heart makes,
but a wet wish her zippity doo-dah craves,
he wants to bite her like a juicy, waxed apple,
even if she's poisonous, even if he knows,
someday her prince will come inside her,
but until then, Sexy is her tour guide beyond
castle walls, how he can tongue his way into
her Storybook, show her more than Sleepy,
Sneezy, Grumpy, Happy, Bashful, Dopey,
Doc can ever bestow upon her, more than
off to work we go, how he could go to work
on her, get her off with a whistle while he
whispers, "Hi, ho," he'd hum, she'd blush
like the lips of the Enchanted Rose, he, her
silly beast of a gentleman unfolding his map
of attractions, Fantasyland into Frontierland
curved into the hips of Adventureland, he
would hold her hand, protect her from pirates,
ghosts, hippopotamuses, buy her mint juleps,
get her all wet from the long drop splash,
pictures of open-mouth excitement, fact of
the matter, horniness leads to the fastrack
of Fantasmic orgasms, and no matter what
Tomorrowland brings, space, wars, any land,
any planet, she will always be the fairest one
of all, a thousand times fairer than any Disney
singing bird's voice, even a glass coffin
couldn't enclose the life of her beauty, the off
chance, the grim chance she is left alone, ever,
Sexy will bring her back to the mirror.

Undressing Victoria Lucas

"Woman is but an engine of ecstasy..." —*Sylvia Plath*

Before the bell jar breaks,
I will not tread upon you
with yellow eyes of a panther
coming up the stairs,
I will meet you at the bottom curl,
trace the Victorian rail's
soft, glossy spine,
offer my cup of calm lust,
your pendant shining over your heart,
complementary to your eyes' touch,
like an impulsive smile
photographed by an enamored stranger,
each wood step, a haunted creaking door,
a decision from the kitchen to the bedroom
that a birthday wish does not become
a death wish, staircase left behind
to pull back ghost white sheets,
to surrender beyond nakedness,
amaranth sweater taken over head,
bra straps slipped off dipped shoulders,
hairclip fallen to the floor,
no longer the mirror of a past poem,
silver, exact, expression the reflection
of truth, four-cornered like walls
and manuscript confessions
for decorated darkness, no frills,
no preconceptions, no glory box,
heaven nor hell, only the body
of vulnerability knocking
the glass dome from the nightstand
to shatter into pieces at your bare feet,
I will be there to sweep the shards away
in the morning, place a finger to your lips

as the sun undresses the moon,
that old, primitive urge for survival
like you once told yourself, no more
words, no flowers for the table,
for your grave, the dead bell,
a hollow toll to answer.

Painting of a Female Joker

I helped you rearrange, declutter,
drag the desk out, move mirrors,
your mother's clock, your father's
Vietnam picture, your swap meet
painting of a female joker, hung
it in your apartment dining room
above the AC wall unit, the idea
of it being fun, fierce, badass,
Harley Quinn, Batman's titted
nemesis gripping a sharp, bloody
knife, her own self-image poker
card burning between two fingers,
hair a chemical green, grin
extended into makeup deliberately
toxic, as days and months passed,
every time I looked at it, where
we ate our oatmeal and eggs,
drank beers, played cards, games,
laid out puzzles too difficult
to finish, where we painted our
own canvases under the influence
of a late-night's drunken, smoky
nakedness, your serene, sandy
beach reflection, my amateur
interpretation of death, you taught
me to use complementary tones,
blues, reds, yellows, purples, we
tacked and balanced our paintings
on each side of the mirror over
the dining table, they seemed to hold
us together in our differences, but
more and more, whenever I'd come
by to pick you up or spend the night,
it was the painting of a female joker
that became the first face I'd see

when I entered the front door, you'd
be in the bathroom getting ready,
putting on your own makeup, I'd
sit on the couch and wait as it crept
in my mind, I'd wonder if it crossed
in yours, how you were adamant
about not taking it down, it felt like
her eyes and smeared smile became
yours, did you envision yourself
as her maybe without even realizing
it, I should have noticed that look
of mischievous foreshadowing,
that villainous approach to love.

Blue Note Reflections

—after *Speak No Evil*, Wayne Shorter

Her image appears at the hotel bar,
vampish, porcelain face
captured in an electric glow,
like a Hollywood, retro photograph,
lipsticked lips
that could leave an indelible imprint
on a nightstand letter,
mascaraed eyes
that can make anyone feel
like a lonely man on a business trip,
no talk, but cocktails,
body language, bedroom glances,
eyes telling each other what's
about to go down, elevator mirrors
going up, opening to noir shadows,
a Hyacinth-papered hallway,
champagne on ice poured
into glass kiss sentiments,
sipped and slipped like sapphire
in and out of my grasp,
life and death in her possession,
how her evil, wild flower perfume
compliments her midnight garden,
hotel sign flashing outside
like her unveiled spell, a jazz
between sheets, we play each other
like piano keys, drum beats,
sax, the after-scent of sex
and cigarettes, traces lingering
like a dream from the bed
translucent to the Vorhang Curtain,
her vision at the balcony window;
the coming of blue note reflections,
smoking, nude figure vanishing
in the indigo light of morning.

Used Mouthpiece

—after the song, "Saxophone," by The Piranhas

Sharp cut of love in a growling night,
I remember your shiny, lipstick ligature,
cool body curved like a nice piece of brass,
your French horniness,
my mouth and fingers to you after bourbon,
positioning for a multitude of touch,
both of us impassioned in a bedded glissando,
repeated slap tonguing,
your licked embouchure,
bell ringing, you opened your lips,
both hands wrapped around my sax,
your throat placement warming up and down
the staff, reading soft, sexy measures,
long, hard, staccato, vibrato of the jaw,
breathy fallouts, you played
until I wanted only you, instrumentalists
to one another's instruments, crescendo
into euphoric climax, you put me away
in the torn lining of lust's case,
restless yearn and tempt,
how I want to be played again and again.

Variations of V

She sucked me like a quantum vacuum.
I invaded her like an 80s alien-lizard
TV miniseries;
intentions of love
lacking verisimilitude,
when opening up and revealing
becomes invention,
ever so slowly, so lonely,
and it's over like a mirrored casket burial,
to move on, across stepping stones of tombs,
divinity in a dark cloud
waiting for velocity's return,
to be alive
without envy, to be back
craving, scratching, grasping
the vernacular of bedded passion,
oh yes, oh god, oh fuck—into the vortex,
the ventriloquistic heart,
the vertical spread,
the voluptuous
void.

Writer's S&M

When I spank the laptop keys a little harder
to show a poem which one of us is wearing the collar,
that high-heeled bitch breaks out the leather whip,
shoves a gag ball in my mouth and calls me a nasty
poetic slave, then for kicks, presses her stiletto
to my balls and what is then heard in my head
is my own screaming grunt, like a Sasquatch fucking
a raccoon, and the nympho cunt muse really likes this—
the sound of the animal experiencing some sort of
erotic torture, it thinks that I like this, this pleasure
through pain, and perhaps I do to an extent, I've grown
accustomed to the *no pain, no gain* mantra, it's how
I get through each day; if I'm not numb, I'm in some
sort of orgasmic misery, though I'd prefer not to have
my testicles stepped on. I need those like Newton's
Cradle and as long as I don't have to give up my swing
set to the writing process, then the dominatrix of poetry
can run the Wartenberg Wheel's shiny spikes up my
spine to my medulla oblongata, over my Adam's apple,
down my treasure line, it's all fine and dandy. I can
endure and lash back. I've got an inflatable sex pillow
for lumbar support. I've got computer drives as hard
and floppy as giant dildos, I've got a mind like a
lubricated fist that's clinched and ready to slide in
and out, internal and end rhymes, I have alliteration
and assonance to be kissed, metaphors to insert like
spreader bars for the Strappado, I can mount falling
meter into rising, penetrating meter, I can get extremely
anal with my editing, locking syllables like handcuffs
and nipple clamps all while giving literal and clitoral
stimulation simultaneously blindfolded. Who's your
daddy now, bitch?! I am. Even when I'm chained
to St. Andrew's Cross looking like a human *X marks
the spot*, I will be in the back of your throat and the front
of your thoughts. I am the writer and she is my tool
and when the game is coming to a climax, just remember
this, when I bring out the gimp, it'll be all over.

Other Than Jazz or Drugs

When I see the word experimental,
I think of an adolescent game;
playing doctor in the dog house
with the girl next door... and later
in life, an adult male pumping blindly
into a woman who breathes a hot,
fake *yes*! as he comes without a clue
as to where in that Bermuda Triangle
of lost souls is the location
of that fucking G-spot?

I think of cloned sheep, the mating
of broccoli and cauliflower,
Philadelphia, Dr. Frankenstein,
Michael Jackson, imitation crab,
and the inventors of SPAM.

I think of a party host serving chains
and whips next to the chip and dip bowl.

I think of a poet named Lisa
pouring burning wax on my nipples,
then blowing the candle's flame
into smoke and handing it to her artist
of a husband who dips the wick
into a thimble of vermillion
and paints me as a statue
of pain and pleasure.

I also think some experiments go too far.

Future Poetry

Particle I
Strap on your VR
helmet. Eye scroll
down to select
a category. There
it is, Poetry. No,
you passed it you
pervert. Not Porn.
OK, Poetry will
wait for you.

Particle II
Like a hot, lovely
tongue in your ear
or the insertion
of Khan's eels.

Particle III
Satellite pings are
related to bongos
of the past. A turtle-
necked alien vapes
an O. It was poison.
It was beaten and
sputtered. A black
beret rests on the
hip of Rasputin.

Particle IV
Oregon does not
resemble an organ
or a gun.

Particle V
Wehvcum2probeuranus

What is Poetry?

A
E
I
O
U
and sometimes Y

T
I
T
S
poem done.

The Art of Pissing in Duchamp's *Fountain*

Do not try this into the wind.
Do not flip three coins while seeking happiness.
Do not eat asparagus!
This is not a toilet (anymore)
since 1917,
this is not a pipe, nor a dream, Nora Barnacle,
James Joyce partook in a flushed flog
per modern day sources and leftover saucepans,
this is after the before was the beginning of

the art of not,
the not of art,
the art of art,
the not of not,

J.D., gulp, Salinger
caught the "yellow" fever in his future,
according to his daughter in a used library book,
just another "golden" tangent,
hypothetically, to the previous previous,
don't worry,

I didn't eat a spear, my dear, but I hear
Brian Eno in a French interview
leaked his method
during a museum lecture in 1990,
snuck a long tube in his pants, (yes,
happy to see you if you were there),

                                    wink wink,

premeditated pee pee
siphoned through an opening of security
glass encasement, drips dropped
into the unflushable abode,

                                    can I say,

R. Mutt meets R. Kelly,

can I get an Amen,
can I get an *en garde*, avante-garde,
can I get a present day air freshener?

Workofart

Silence   is important,

but space
                    is probably more;

we need to breathe   in relationships,
in design, in elevators, in language,
sometimes,
                    whenwordsarepressedtogether,

a scriptio continua,   doesn't   quite
look   right,
when a repellant word appears
that can turn
            a work of art into a deadly turnoff.

In poetry,
you just don't go there. Nobody wants to see
or hear the makings of that   other F word—

fart.
                    Maybe *old fart* is okay,
when you're poking fun at your aging father,
but not an ass fart.   You just can't make
an ass fart sexy. You can't make it beautiful.
A fart is not made to allure, unless you have
a certain fetish for foul play.

You can, however, make it   the butt
of a joke,   but
that's   so   low   brow,
        a totally unpleasant crop dust aroma
over the entire art community,
which makes me wonder, how low can you
                            go,
                    a pull-my-
finger poem, is a fart the lowest denominator?

Magician's Book of One-Liners

You can call me David, David Copafeel.

I've got a weenie like Houdini.
You could have the trunk I can't escape from.

When I saw your box, I saw your better half.

Look closely. There's nothing up my sleeve,
but there's something up yours.

With a wave of my magic wand, I can make
a tiger vanish into thin air. But who gives a fuck
about tigers, open sesame.

My lovely assistants, repeat after me, Hocus
Pocus Faster.

Before this handkerchief becomes a dove,
I'm going to need it to clean up my act.

And Presto! I take the silver coins from behind
your earlobes and replace them with your legs.

I can catch a bullet with my teeth.
You should see what I can do with my tongue!

For my final trick, watch me pull something else
other than the rabbit out.

Thanks for coming, I hope you enjoyed the show.

Never Open With the Weather (Writing Rule #1)

The promiscuous dusk was female moist,
(consequently,
moist, the most hated word in the English language,
yet even though it's how to describe
the perfect texture for a cupcake,
"This is really moist!" one would kindly articulate
at someone's birthday party)
the promiscuous dusk was cupcake-ish?

Suddenly, All Hell Broke Loose!!!

—In response to Elmore Leonard's *10 Rules of Writing*

Rule #1
Never open a book with the weather
and so, with an impending tentacle of Technicolor,
bloodletting sunset, the red velvet cupcake moist
wind out of the west, blew pages of the book like
a bad blowjob.

Rule #2
Avoid Prologues
Prologue 1: (technically, there is no such thing as
a bad blowjob)
Prologue 2: (oh wait, teeth)
Prologue 3: (sneezing and hiccups)
Prologue 4: (blue balls)
Prologue 5: (I should have listened to Elmore)
Prologue 6: (I believe air is plurality, a multitude
of ominous foretelling. It's going to get dark and
wet. Lives will be lost while one man finds
pleasure in fallen, kinky nakedness)
Prologue 7: (I opened the book at the mall so as
to avoid the weather, but the prologues were unavoidable)

Rule #3
Never use a verb other than "said" to carry dialogue
I surmise, "I'm too sexy for this rule," and I reckon,
"Rules are meant to be broken," and here we are,
hypothesizing, "Right Said Fred is not a verb."

Rule #4
Never use an adverb to modify the verb "said"
I underhandedly said, "Fuck it!"

Rule #5
Keep your exclamation points under control!
But! What if I stub my toe!! Or get road rage!!!
Or hit the jackpot!!!! Or I'm about to cum!!!!

Rule #6
Never use the words "suddenly" or "all hell broke loose"
See what I did there with the title?

Rule #7
Use regional dialect, patois, sparingly
Like, this rule is grody to the max, for sure,
totally doesn't pertain to like, California, right?

Rule #8
Avoid detailed descriptions of characters
She was cupcake moist, he was poundcake horny.
Isn't it all in the details?

Rule #9
Same for places and things
After being born in a Wolfgang Puck's restaurant
in Los Angeles, California, as his mother was
induced into labor after sucking down a spicy,
Sweet Fennel Sausage Pizza, Barry was born a
writer. Then, Whammo! Naked Japanese!

Rule #10
Leave out parts readers tend to skip
Ghost-faced unexpectedly, "Shit, oh fucking shit!"
when Barry sees and hears surrealistically from
across the street of the Japanese love hotel,
the shattering of the ninth floor window just under
the cherry-blossom pink and electric blue neon pair
of jumping dolphins, a petite, disheveled school girl
with side tails and glow-in-the-dark dildo protruding
out of her asshole, crashes through the glass, blood
squirting from her legs wrapped around a businessman

in his fifties wearing only a black necktie with white
polka dots, still engaged in coitus, screaming out
"Eeee!" and "Ohhh!" That's when Barry started
snapping pictures, about halfway down, the plunging
couple in the midst of an epic climax. "At least he's
going out on top," Barry chuckled philosophically
as he went back to his book, noticing the front cover,
a photographer posed in a voyeuristic aim at the reader,
words on the camera lens stating, *Made in Japan.*
Barry could not believe the irony. "How it all comes
together," he breathed, the two bodies bouncing off
the sidewalk like water balloons, dildo launching
into the air, caught in an accelerating wind, moved
across the street like a serpentine apparition
of a sperm, swirling over Barry's head.

An Unusual Way to Clap at a Poetry Reading

The poem ended
and the audience started their applause,
I happened to look across the room,
saw a woman clapping like I have never seen
anyone clap before,
she didn't use two hands,
she was holding something in one of them,
a water bottle or maybe the smartphone
she had been staring at throughout the poem,
instead of setting the item down to put
two hands together or just smile
and nod or tap a knee or stomp a foot
to make noise, she took her free hand,
went across her chest and clapped a titty,
her left hand to her big, right boob, to be exact,
and it wasn't a soft pat, it was legitimate,
harder than trying to make a baby burp,
it was closer to hitting a restaurant choker
on the back to get a cocktail shrimp
out of a throat, I mean, her tit took it
like a heavyweight champ absorbs a punch,
and in an unusual way, I applaud her
for her on-the-spot grit, lazy or inventive
or masochistic as it was, I'm giving
a one-handed ovation at the computer desk,
but I'm not going to clap a nut.

L.A. Make-Out Interrupted

Oh Highland Park,
I can hear it clear as day
still hocking in my ear,
in the little parking lot
after tacos and poetry,
a congested stranger
clearing out a mass
of mucous from
the back of his throat.
We stood by her car,
engaged in wet kissing,
our tongues and lips
turning into dumbfounded
laughter, mood
breaking like a belch
at an opera, a dark, curly
hair in the sour cream
of our carne asada fries.
We shook it off,
this gross proclamation,
as best we could,
reconnected our mouths
for another round
of make-out, until
a minute later, a second
loogie. This guy
and his repeat offender
throat; the epitome
of the unmannered
public. No regard
for the outside world,
our little place of desire
for privacy, swapping
paradox of PDA
and lasting goodbyes.

Better Than Sex

Some say there are things
like cake, like death, books,
cigarettes, Lucky Charms,
nachos, breakfast burritos,
pizza, chocolate anything,
burgers, fries, bacon, beer,
wine, whiskey, music,
sleep, moisturizer? What
is it that makes it better?
Do necessities count, like
relieving your bladder
when you have to pee
like a diuretic racehorse?
Does pissing count as
trumping sex? Is a golden
shower a double trump,
does sex overrule humiliation?
Is the 8-12 hertz of alpha
waves while playing Tetris,
fitting a block strategically
into a space, beat sticking
a cock into a slot. When
you Netflix and chill, what if
you never get to the chill
because the binge-watching
bug bites you harder?
Would I rather be tapped
into writing a poem than
tapping that ass? Is a hole
just a hole to fill, what could
fill a hole better than sex,
or does it depend on who
you are having sex with?

Brazil Butt Lift Poem

It was a combination of boredom,
random South American curiosity,
a fascination for infomercials
like the Shake Weight,
the Snuggie, the ShamWow,
Ginsu, the no!no!,
that caused me to channel past
Chopped and a rerun of Seinfeld,
to discover what this
Brazil Butt Lift was all about.
Six kickass videos, instant access
to the Bum Bum Rapido workout,
dance, cardio, sculpting,
full gluteus Triangle Training
of medius, maximus, and minimus,
a total buttocks transformation system
designed by Portuguese accented,
sun tanned, blue eyed, stubble faced,
self-proclaimed "Brazilian Butt Master,"
Leandro. One testimonial says
your butt will look like a little apple.
Just call 1 (800) 499-5051
and make 4 easy payments of $19.95,
they'll even throw in free
booty shorts and makeover calendar.
Check out my sexy butt now.

Red Wine Review

Even though I'm in
my Walmart loungewear
in front of the computer
amidst swirls
of Glade air freshener
and 94.7
The Wave sax melodies,
I feel sophisticated,
like a Blue Note
jazz collector,
or the son of a sommelier,
about to feel
the low budget buzz
from a late night pour
of Chalk Creek;
and immediately,
I am intrigued
by the Cabernet cascade—
a melted piece
of stained glass
church window
held up to the light,
then to my nose,
the Mendocino wine
opens like a lotus flower,
emitting hints of
Snickerdoodles,
Christmas potpourri,
Cuban cigar boxes,
Playdough rainbows,
lap dances in Vegas.
That's when I sense
this vintage possesses
the body, the legs,
and the finish, too.

With a sip, with a cheek
to cheek swish,
it seems like I'm rinsing
my mouth with
a millionaire's Listerine.
But this isn't a gargle,
this is steak juice
running into mashed
potatoes, this is milk
at the end of a bowl
of Fruit Loops,
this is the date who
doesn't want to be
dropped off after dinner,
who stays and leaves
the bottle uncorked,
the scent of her
perfume on the pillow
the next morning.

Slather

Knives cut
both bread and throats,
when I look past your eyes,
grab the handle,
you are already stabbed
and cooked deep
from previous trips to butchers
and bakers, I'm just
the candlestick maker, baby,
no slicing any of you,
only want to light your way,
wax poetic against the walls,
dinner with a flicker
and shadowdance, drip
down our time spent,
strip and breadsticks
for the purpose of eating,
I know how to dip
my wick and I know
how to use a knife,
but I would rather lather
with it, not cut,
but coat your throat
with my name, spread it
across your artisan skin
like warm butter,
melt and cool
to the shape of your
Machete
curves,
you
ahead
of me,
sealed,
scented,
sloppy,
slathered.

Nude Ascending a Staircase

—after *Nude Descending a Staircase*,
oil painting by Marcel Duchamp

Coming from the cool fridge,
goosed skin, taut nipples,
a glass of Rosé and baguette,
a barefoot slide across the dust
of scraped maple wood—
nude ascending, a conjunction
of hips and limbs, like
simultaneous possession
of demon and lover, body
mimicking deconstructed
patterns, inhabited hourglass
of sex and time, a staircase
continuum elapsed in
juxtaposition to another *Nude*
on the staircase wall, ancestor
of oiled flesh permutations,
woman walking, man walking
to the understanding of the bed,
to the movement of fucking
on top of one another,
dreams of space, not of stars,
but a freeness, descension/
ascension into climax,
all the canvas of the inside.

Erotic Topography

Across the flat, MDF square,
you press your fingers firm
along the surface of the board,
30 grit sandpaper coarsely grinding,
tracing penciled lines and curves
to shape an architectural landscape
into your expression of the erotic—
sawdust on your hands and knees,
you wipe the dirty sweat dampening
on your brow with the back
of your glove, allow your heavy
breathing to slow its carnal pace
before turning and reaching
for the handsaw and chisel,
the orbital sander, the grinder
and Dremel, tools to help continue
the process of smoothing
and forming, the design within you,
tactile and affectionate,
caressing and refining,
utilizing the higher abrasive
on a contour of wooden waves
to bring about a climactic display
of light and shadow captured,
passion projected in a frame
to be publicly viewed and touched
on the art walls of a gallery,
knowing you are part of nature's
creation, reconstructed into
the future of the earth's terrain.

Nimbus Sunset

She photographs sunsets over ocean waves
to collect healing moments for her walls.
I would be by her side sometimes,
standing in a damp, Hemingway wind
out on a Southern California pier,
taking pictures of hopeful inevitability,
nimbus sheathing sporadic spectrums,
our hooded embraces
trying to keep us warm
while eating ice cream, while stormy
pasts loom present island beings,
sunset offering contemplative chances,
time to escape, or attempt,
like two bodies pulsing into a sleeping
spoon, dreams drifting and rafting
in the wake-up to a sweet delusion.
My heart tells me the truth inside—
for her, no metaphor exists
that doesn't linger, her blood kiss
like the ocean of the sky,
a drowning and healing, prayers
for a vast horizon to unhook
the unwilling, uncertain vulnerability,
questions breeding nature's theories,
the relativity of love,
the paradox of Pandora's box; she
opened me up
and I let go of myself too much,
a beautiful, opaque ocean of fears
in a whirlpool with desire,
stardust on the verge, night urging
the lover's search for sheltered
pleasure clouded by another day,
heartbreak for her sunset.

Neruda in the Bermuda Triangle

The
signal has
disappeared and
I am left circling with
a collection of love poems,
an early edition, tattered Neruda
given to me by a past lover, cover torn,
pages stained like aged nicotine, bittersweet
scent spread to my face, reminiscent of our after-
hours world, when desire was a mapless course, a blind
seductive fog like the afterbreath of a long, wet kiss, a taste
of cigarette, of found emotions lost under constellations, of a wild,
magnetic spin like the roulette of a corybantic compass, a directionless
inevitable succumbing to nature's fate and the consequential longing, the up-
ward feeling of a downward spiral, hourglass of a whirlpool, inured to the enigmas
of a triangle in a shapeless ocean, sucked by the lips of every remembered kiss, the first
against the parked car of night, another to bring her back again, before she vanishes, before
all transmission is a lost cause, if you can hear me even if it's over, *I am that net waiting emptily*
—*out of range*, I loved you in a stranded void, I am left here circling with a collection of love poems.

ACKNOWLEDGEMENTS

For everyone who has ever supported me, inspired me, challenged me on personal and academic levels, thank you for being a part of my poetic journey. The irony of *Suddenly, All Hell Broke Loose!!!* is in the word, suddenly, for in actuality, there have been many years and experiences spent on crafting poetry, let alone building up a body of work. In my case, I attribute certain elements of my poetry to the following: the music in my poetry to my grandpa Kenny, beginning with sitting in front of the walnut stereo cabinet he built, listening to vinyl records of orchestras, developing an ear for rhythm; my appreciation of words and language was afforded to me through my mother Sylvia, and my grandma Margie encouraging me to write; the humor of my poetry, to listening to the insightful, filthy comedians who provided me with hours of laughs and entertainment; the passionate nature of my poetry to becoming an intellectual animal, a sexual being, a collective heart, and for help in refining my poetry, to the academic/crafting stage in the MFA Creative Writing program at Cal State University, Long Beach, and continuing hereafter with writing, contemplating, procrastinating, documenting life's wild ride, random everyday wacky, mundane, lustful, blissful, tragic, magic moments. To my mentors at CSULB, Charles Harper Webb and Gerald Locklin, I owe much gratitude. To my poetry community, thank you for the years of friendship and workshops, more especially, Ja'net, Jhoanna, and Kathryn. This particular collection of poems would not have come together without the titillating interest, and unwavering love of Shannon Phillips at Picture Show Press. Also, to my family, who listened to me read out my words. To my friends, old and new, interested parties inside and outside the world of poetry, this is a way out and a way in, a way to break loose! Let's give em' hell! Much love and thanks.

Brian Harman was born and raised in Orange County, California, where he can be found trying new craft beers, creating themed playlists, and rooting for the Angels. His work has been published in *Chiron Review*, *Nerve Cowboy*, *Misfit Magazine*, and elsewhere. His poetry mentors include Gerald Locklin and Charles Harper Webb.

www.ingramcontent.com/pod-product-compliance
Lightning Source LLC
Chambersburg PA
CBHW071738020426
42331CB00008B/2077